My Story:

Athlete Edition

Table of contents

Chapter 1- Mindset of an elite athlete

In all stages of being an athlete from beginning to end there is some component or 6th sense if you will. I can remember somewhere around the 6th or 7th grade I would roll out my roll-away goal and shoot 1000 shots in 106 degree heat in Kansas City, Missouri. At the time I was just shooting because I hated missing shots. I would shoot left hand layups and trick shots just to have fun and then I would shoot free throws, putting myself in extreme game situations with us (imagining) winning or losing on my make or miss. After that the other kids would be getting home around five or six in the evening and we would play games until there was no light left or everyone left to go home. I guess what I'm trying to say is that nobody made me do those things, or suggested that I did those things. It was just something in me that forced me in that direction similar to how a bird automatically knows to fly south during winter.

     As I grew more and more into an athlete, so did my competitive nature. I hated to lose, or to not be chosen, or even for someone to say that someone else was better than I was. Not from a jealous perspective but it was pure competitive nature that if I had a say in it, not only am I better than you but I'm willing to die to prove it. In my mind; you may be taller, faster, stronger or even more talented than I was but you will never outwork me on any level. That same personality trait took me everywhere that I wanted to be from a sports perspective and some places that I didn't want to be as well.

I was a second generation athlete and at the time I didn't even know. My father was a star football player in high school, college and even made it pro playing for the Houston Oilers, Kansas City Chiefs and a few other professional teams. He told me how he was raised on a farm, and that in itself takes being an athlete to a different level. He would wake up in the morning and run a few miles, do push-ups and sit-ups and other exercises then do the early morning farm work. After that he would shower and get ready for school only to have practice after school in whatever sport he was playing depending on the season. I remember asking him one time "why did you wake up early before farm work just to work-out"? His response was the same reply in my mind that all elite athletes would or should have, he said "you have to always be in shape mentally and physically because there is always someone else out there working twice as hard as you are". What I took away from what he was saying is that being a regular athlete is physical, however being an elite athlete was all mental or at least more mental than anything else.

"AS AN ELITE LEVEL ATHLETE, YOU TRAIN SO INTENSE AND SO HARD (OUTSIDE OF PRACTICE) THAT PRACTICE AND EVEN GAMES ARE EASY. WHEN YOU LOOK ACROSS AT YOUR OPPONENT YOU KNOW THAT YOU HAVE TRAINED HARDER THAN HIM OR HER FOR LONGER THAN HIM OR HER ALL YEAR ROUND AND TO TAKE IT TO A DEEPER LEVEL I CAN ALMOST GUARANTEE THAT WITH ANY OF THE GREATS IN ANY SPORT OR

ENDEAVOR FOR THAT MATTER THAT THEY WILL SAY IT'S NOT EVEN REALLY ABOUT YOUR OPPONENT, IT IS ALWAYS YOU VS. YOU." Maurice King

Here is a post about the two of us in the Amarillo Globe Newspaper.

Plainview's King learning the ropes from his father

Posted: Tuesday, August 29, 2000

LANCE LAHNERT
Globe-News Sports Writer

Long before Plainview's Maurice King wreaked havoc on the football field in Bulldog Stadium, a family member was doing the same about 60 miles up Interstate 27 at Kimbrough Memorial Stadium.

Lockney native Danny Clark, King's dad, was a standout running back for West Texas State between 1978-81. Clark's dazzling ability to run netted him 23 career touchdowns, ranking him 10th on the Buffs' all-time scoring list.

Even with this football background, Maurice King didn't grow up as an eat/breath/sleep football kid.

"Basketball is my passion," King said. "Really, though, during whatever season I'm playing, I love that sport more than anything else. I've always been the type of person to where you tell me what you want done, I will get it done for you."

Second-year Plainview coach Marty McClintock likes what he sees in his 6-foot-4, 215-pound senior defensive tackle.

"Maurice can dominate the defensive line of scrimmage," McClintock said. "He is so tall and has a reach that allows him to reach around defenders and do things you can't normally get away with. Maurice's role is to wreak havoc. He does, too."

It didn't appear likely three years ago King would help anchor the Bulldogs defensive line at weak-side tackle - one of the key roles in Plainview's scheme.

Until last August, King was a student at Grandview High in Kansas City, Mo.

"I was living with my sister," King said. "Since about the seventh grade my parents have been wanting to move to Plainview. It has turned out the best for me."

King arrived at Plainview High two weeks into the 1999-2000 school year. By the fifth game of the football season against Pampa, he was in the lineup.

"They like football up there in Kansas City," King said. "But in Texas, I mean these people go all out for football."

Almost every day this past summer, King was working out by 6 a.m., "going through my father's own little training camp." King would run sprints, go for a 12-minute jog, crank out 100 push-ups and 100 sit-ups, then get behind a 1998 Dodge Ram truck.

Not the steering wheel.

"My dad would find some flat ground, then put the truck in neutral," King said. "I would get behind the truck and push it between 50 and 60 yards. He told me when we started, 'Son, you are going to hate me for this while I'm doing this. But during the football season when you get tired, you will be able to go that extra mile.' "

Things to think about

1. What are your short and long term goals?
2. What do you do everyday in pursuit of those goals?
3. What are you willing to sacrifice to obtain those goals?

Chapter 2- Where it all began

My Journey athletically started about 5th grade. I was decent in basketball and football or anything else for that matter but I had never played any organized sport before. My first organized sport was football or South Suburban football as we call it here in Kansas City. It is the equivalent of what others call "pop warner" or "peewee league". My first football coach was Coach Kahlil and Coach Rupe. I can remember having to run to the backstop and back for conditioning and since I was new to sports in an organized way, I was also new to this conditioning. I hated it (out of shape) but my coaches found a way to make us mentally get through it all. That was my first lesson in mental toughness for both life and sports.

Coach Kahlil used to tell us that life and sports go hand-in-hand and that sports was the best way to learn life because in sports there will always be another practice or game but in life you get one chance. I can honestly say that when I first started I was big but that was it. I was what you call soft or nice. There was a monster in there, I had just never tapped into it before and the moment I did was a life defining moment for me. That was the moment where I realized that I can handle mental and physical pain, and also the moment that I realized I can go to a different level at any time I chose to and that ability is a must to be an athlete. Again I never really trained to play football until my senior year in high school, it had always come natural to me and while I honestly wasn't an all-star my first year playing football, I learned several valuable lessons in life. After south suburban football was over then of course came south suburban basketball. Many of the same players and coaches that coached or played in football were there again in basketball too.

Now here is where my story hits new lows and highs and gets a little interesting. The majority of the kids in both football and basketball had been playing organized sports for at least 2-3 years or more before I had, so they had experience of how things worked as well as playing experience. I was the "King" at recess playing against far less athletic kids but I was neutralized when I decided to play for the first time in a league that went deeper than sports, it was life for these coaches who I'm sure had coaching or playing dreams at some point and hundreds of kids who at least in their mind would play professionally one day. My first basketball coach was coach Ronnie Morris of the Kansas City Heat. Again I was just big and didn't have any real skill other than playing at recess or for fun. It was a situation where I played only because my mom paid and the rules where I had to at least touch the floor I believe one minute per half. And to top it off, I was in the middle of a growth spurt at the time so I was always tripping over my feet and I spent more time on the floor than a mop. It was ugly, but again I learned several lessons that season that I still carry with me today. Now here specifically is the moment that changed my life both as an athlete and person but ultimately the direction of my life and God-Given ability. At the end of the south suburban season Coach Ronnie was handing out papers to what seemed like everyone but I'm sure there were a few who didn't receive them. These papers were for the AAU team that Coach Ronnie coached every year and that was real deal. I can till this very day remember it so vividly, as coach gave papers to the two or three people before me and then gave a paper to a few more people and then the practice and season was over. I went up to coach and said "hey Coach Ronnie, you forgot to give me one". He turned to me and said Slam (that was my nickname due to the fact we had two Maurice's on the team) I didn't forget, you didn't make the cut. That was the moment that changed me for the rest of my life. At that very moment I promised myself that I would get every paper that was given out from that moment forward. Sometimes I wonder if Coach Ronnie was doing that strategically because he knew exactly what it would trigger in me, or was I just that terrible. I went home, I didn't say a word to my mother on the way home which was weird because she would always talk the entire ride home, or sing loudly like she was the only person in the car. The mixture of feelings that I had at that moment were like a split second of sadness then an eternity of what I like to call the perfect storm. I was never mad or upset with Coach Ronnie but again as an athlete, not getting picked or not being good enough did something to me. That very next day after school I went to work. I worked on left hand finishes and dribbling and I also worked in an unorthodox manner on my jump shot. At the apartments we lived in, there was covered parking which was about 9 and a half feet tall or so. I would dribble and drive and the front of the covered parking was the imaginary basket. I had to be spot on because too short or air-ball then I would hit someone's car, too high and I lost my ball as there was no getting up there to get it back. I watched film as if I got paid to do it, I studied my favorite players and there moves. I was so focused it was unreal. My life was dedicated to training outside of practice to my new love (basketball).

After a good second season of football, here we are again at basketball season. For whatever reason I ended up back on Coach Ronnie's team again, I'm not sure if he picked me or it was luck of the draw or even if he was happy about it but none the less there I was and this time I would get my paper. Seemingly out of my first growth spurt I was much better and I began to at least get some recognition for now being an athlete. I literally worked my butt off between the previous season and the current season. I could finish with both hands and the fact that I was big I could finish with contact. I can remember hearing one of my best friends grandmother say "Slam isn't flashy and all that, but if you want to score, get slam the ball he'll get it in there". To make a long story short, I got my paper that time and tasted for the first time the fruits of my labor being an athlete. That feeling of having to work to be good was something that I can't explain, something that overtook my heart, mind and soul and I literally became addicted to that feeling. We traveled to places like Detroit, Iowa and Ohio and played players from all over the United States. It's one thing to be pretty good locally but to have never travelled outside of Kansas City playing a sport and seeing the great talent that the world had to offer only grew me up even more. And now I'm officially an athlete.

My thoughts- "I had no idea when I first started playing sports that it would take me to places that it eventually took me. When I first started I honestly sucked which is normal when it comes to something that you are doing for the first time. I worked day and night on just becoming good enough to make the team however that same work ethic eventually took me to not only making the team but pretty much starting for every team I ever played for after that.

"YOU HAVE TO REMEMBER THAT HARD WORK WILL ALWAYS BEAT TALENT WHEN TALENT DOESN'T WORK HARD" Maurice King

Plainview (15-4, 1-0) countered with a strong interior game. The Bulldogs kept dumping the ball inside where Maurice King and Bryson Davis wreaked havoc. King hit his first seven field goals and ended up with 20 points on 9-of-11 shooting, while Davis tossed in 13 points

Things to think about

1. What's your driving force and motivation?
2. If you could do one thing for the rest of your life, what would it be?
3. What are your strengths and weaknesses?
4. How often do you work on your weaknesses and polish your strengths?

Chapter 3- God Gifted

We'll take this story to 7th grade where I now had an identity as a basketball player and football player. I stood about 6'2" and weighed over 200 pounds. In the bible it says that your gifts will make room for you. I was a pretty good basketball player at this time but I was a great football player. Outside of football practice I never worked on anything pertaining to the game of football. I was naturally quick off of the ball and had a nose for the ball as well meaning that I find who had the ball and get to him even if I had to take a few people with me. There were times when I got to the quarterback before or as soon as he got the ball, and there were also times where I didn't know if the running back or the quarterback had the ball so I would tackle them both. Coaches and teammates loved that. I'm in no way bragging or boasting on my ability but only making the point that I was given football by God as one of my gifts. The things that a lot of players had to work on, and define and polish came very naturally to me at a very young age. The crazy part is that I didn't even realize it at the time. I just played football to pass the time until it was basketball season.

There was always an eternal war going on inside of me from the moment when I didn't make my first AAU team. In my mind and heart I was a basketball player and that's all there was to it as far as I was concerned. I think in some crazy way I still had something to prove. I played the game with a chip on my shoulder and I didn't know what the chip was, I just always felt as if I had something to prove at all times. Being a football player made me tougher on a different level than a lot of basketball players. I loved contact, and for the most part I was going to win any body-to- body contests that happen on the basketball court. This I believe made me appealing to a lot of AAU coaches around here. I was pretty good size, and I loved to be physical down low to the point where I was 4, 5, or 6 inches shorter than the person guarding me but I was pushing people around the way that you would want a middle school center or forward to do. There wasn't a doubt in my mind that I wouldn't get a scholarship to a D1 college to be a forward or center and wreak havoc like I was starting to now do on the basketball court. There was only one thing wrong with this picture, I would have to grow another 7 or 8 inches or more to be able to accomplish this. That was never in God's plans for me to do, but I didn't know that at the time and even If I did know that, I would have denied it with a straight face. Here I am 6'2" 230 pounds and already the size of some professional football players, trying to pray that I would grow to be 6'10" so that I could be a basketball player. Long story short, God gave me football, but I always chose basketball.

My thoughts- "When it comes to finding yourself, or your passion or even your purpose, start where you do things great naturally. God gives artists for example great vision almost from birth, and musicians great ears and hearts for music almost from birth. That doesn't mean that you won't have to work on and polish some of these things but what you do greatly and naturally is usually a great start when trying to find and discover who and what you are. For me personally I was a natural athlete that created art on the football field effortlessly and was a pretty good basketball player. While it created an unimaginable work ethic it would come back to haunt me later in life because I didn't listen to what God was telling me."

"ALWAYS START WHERE YOU ARE NATURALLY GIFTED AND WORK FROM THERE, BECAUSE THAT IS WHAT YOU WERE CREATED TO DO" Maurice King

Things to think about

1. What is your passion and what are you naturally gifted at?
2. What is the first thing on your mind when you wake up, and the last thing you think about before you go to sleep?
3. How many hours do you spend (outside of practice) working on your craft?

Chapter 4- Slim&Slam

From almost the beginning of my athletic career I was very close with a person who shared the same name as me and the same love as me for the game of basketball. He was on my first and second basketball teams and we had basically grown up together. We went to the same elementary and middle school and he was an awesome basketball player. When I first started playing the game he was the kid that everyone wanted on their team. He was a tall guard who could also post up and shoot as well. With both of our names being Maurice, Coach Ronnie called him slim and me slam after the twins that played for the University of Missouri during that time period. He was always better than I was, at least at first. He was tall for our age and the skill he possessed was unreal. This was around the 5th through 7th grade, he was the king in my area as far as basketball was concerned. There was not a team that he couldn't play for if he wanted to. Around about the 7th or 8th grade I had fully completed my growth spurt and was also becoming a known and desired basketball player in the area. I could shoot and rebound and was also starting to dunk which was pretty cool. At that time I didn't notice some of the things that were going on. All of a sudden my best friend no longer considered me his best friend, and I never knew why until about 10 or 15 years later. Someone asked me why all of a sudden we had fallen out and weren't friends anymore, I still didn't have an answer for that and I think they asked me this question because they already had an answer for it. I had a work-horse mentality where I believe he felt as if he didn't have to put in the extra hours anymore because he was already a desired talent. It came to the point where now I was the desired talent between the two of us. I had never had him in mind when I was working out and training, the only thing I had in mind was the sour taste of not getting my paper 2 or 3 years prior. That was and still is my driving force to this very day. I had literally went from only playing because the rules stated that I had to, to becoming a person who could pretty much play for any team in the area. Again, I'm in no way bragging about any of that, it was my work ethic off the court that allowed me to be able to play with a lot of the players that I looked up to, and in my mind I never wanted to intentionally out do any of them I just wanted to be able to keep up with them and be respected as a basketball player. But there I go again, being a basketball player in a football player's body. He and I literally never spoke again after that and it became normal even though we still played for the same teams for a while and went to the same schools for a while. In some crazy way though, If it had not been for him initially I probably would have never started playing basketball on an organized level and certainly wouldn't have developed my work ethic as well.

My thoughts- "Sometimes in life people come for a season, but that season has a reason and a purpose. We often times want people to stay in our lives forever but their purpose is to teach us certain things and that is it, and once they have fulfilled their purpose they are gone. In pursuit of greatness and destiny we have to understand that no matter what it is we are striving for be it sports, academics or whatever, some people's roles and positions in our lives are for a short time and are only to prepare us for greater."

"SOMETIMES YOU WALK ALONE, AND LOSE FRIENDS AND EVEN FAMILY ALONG THE WAY TO YOUR DESTINY. FOCUS ON THE END RESULT OF YOUR GOALS AND BE WILLING TO GET THERE EVEN IF IT'S BY YOURSELF."   Maurice King

Things to think about

1. Do your friends and associates align with where you want to go in life?
2. Do your friends feed your destiny or distract you from your destiny?
3. On a scale of 1-10, how would you honestly rate you level of focus? What can you do to change this if it isn't where you need it to be?

Chapter 5- The move

Life continued the same through 8th grade, things were all about AAU ball and school ball meant nothing or at least not as much as AAU ball did. That was about to change fast and drastically going into high school. I remember going from middle school to high school and one of the things that I remember most is now everyone is tall, muscular with mustaches and part-time jobs as I like to joke. Basically these were grown men to me, because in my eyes I was still a little boy. I had not taken the time to look in the mirror and see what outsiders seen. My freshman year at Grandview High School, I stood 6'4" and weighed over 250 pounds. Growing up playing the game on a competitive and organized level it was quite easy to be honest. We went undefeated my freshman year on the freshman team. Coach Knight really enjoyed the talent that he had even though he was the type of man to not let you know how much he enjoyed it. We had Mark Hollins, son of my second basketball coach and Gary White who was a tall athletic shooter as well as Andre Taylor and myself. I remember coach Knight would throw us alley-oops after practice and four of us on the team were dunking so as a coach you can imagine what kind of fun both Coach Knight and we as players had. Sophomore year I played J.V. and Varsity for Coach Don Bickham. He was the coach that you hated until later in life when you finally were at a level mentally to understand what he was trying to instill in you, but at the time he was a no-nonsense kind of coach and I had never experienced anything like him before in my life.

The summer between sophomore and junior year was a life defining moment for me and my career. Looking back I believe God was putting me in the place he wanted me to shine the way he created me to shine with his gift of football. My sister who I was living with because my mom moved to Texas and I didn't want to go, had had enough of my rebellious antics and literally within in 24 hours I was in route to Plainview, Tx. I remember being so homesick it was ridiculous, here I was a city boy from a place where we had malls, and amusement parks and just the regular city lifestyle now in a place where not only did I not know anybody but to me this was the country. You never know what God has planned for you, but it's said that if God orders it he'll pay the bill meaning God in one way or another had it planned for me to move to Texas and he made a way so that his plan for my life could be fulfilled. My dad pre-enrolled me in school and told them about me. By the time that I had gotten there and started school the word was all around town that I could really play football and basketball. I remember my first day there, people thought I was a teacher because of my size. I had grown to 6'5" 285 pounds so I guess I could see why they though that. I was a fish out of water, that was until after my first day of school and my first football practice then for at least a little while it felt like home. Why they put me on the J.V. football team I'll never know but for the first few weeks that's where I was, and honestly it was like being a man amongst boys. They eventually saw that too and immediately moved me to Varsity football. That's when football took on a different meaning and all around look.

They had a 6'4", 220 pound running back by the name of Roderick Ansley who also happened to be the #2 running back in the state and ran a 4:3 40-yard dash, and a 6'3", 260 pound full back by the name of Bryson Davis (who went to Mississippi State) and a slew of other unbelievably massive players who after I proved myself, welcomed me with open arms. I had never been in a town where they basically shut the whole town down to go to the high school games, it blew my mind how serious these people were about their sports and particularly football. I was bound to show them all, what I and my family already knew which was "you want to play football?, ok just let me loose on the field." I think it's safe to say everyone was happy about the move eventually. Here's a post from the local newspaper.

Whatever the case, Plainview toppled Snyder 35-21 Friday in the District 4-4A opener for both teams.

Trailing 14-6 and not moving the ball on offense, the Bulldogs needed a spark to electrify the packed house and their own sideline. Plainview got that spark from an unlikely source defensive tackle Maurice King. The big man intercepted a batted ball on the Bulldog 46 and lumbered 54 yards for the score.

An excessive celebration penalty pushed the Bulldogs back 15 yards on the extra-point attempt, and Plainview was forced to kick. Sergio Zuniga made the kick but Snyder showed a sign of things to come by jumping offsides. Bulldog coach Marty McClintock decided to try for a potential game-tying time two-point conversion, and quarterback Kyle Miller hit Bryson Davis in the flat and let the 244-pound fullback do the rest for a 14-14 halftime deadlock.

"Maurice's interception return and the two-point conversion were a huge lift for us going into the half," McClintock said. "We had some mistakes in the first half, but like this team has done time and time again, they came together and played solid in the second half."

King had actually foreseen the play earlier in the day.

"I told Richard (Gomez) that I was going to this earlier (Friday)," King said. "I told him to bat the ball up in the air and I would take it all the way. Coach told me to make a big play and I was able to."

My thoughts- "Even though I hated every moment and even the thought of moving from my home, God knew what he was doing according to his plan for my life. One thing about being an elite athlete is, if you can play ball then you can play ball. It doesn't matter where, when, or how, you have to be able to adjust to change and just be an elite athlete weather you're in a big city or small town."

"THE ONLY THING THAT WILL NEVER CHANGE IS THE FACT THAT THINGS WILL ALWAYS CHANGE. YOUR SCHOOL, COACHES, TEAMMATES ETC. WILL ALWAYS CHANGE AND YOU STILL HAVE TO BE ELITE AND NOT JUST GO THROUGH THESE CHANGES BUT GROW THROUGH THEM AS WELL." Maurice King

Things to think about

1. What is at that you bring to your craft that nobody else can do the way you do?
2. Do you have an identity outside of your craft and if so what is it?
3. If you couldn't do your craft professionally, what are the top three things you would love to do for the rest of your life?

Chapter 6. - 3.5, 10,3 Vs. 14&8

Now officially a Plainview Bulldog, even though I was still homesick I began to become quite fond of my new surroundings. Plainview was a little different in culture and the way things operated. My first weird experience there is one that I will never forget. My first car was a 1998 Pontiac Grand Am, I loved that car. I was about to get a taste of small town life and big time talent. I was driving after school going somewhere, knowing me I was probably either picking up Ziggy (my best friend at the time and also that 244pound fullback that I was talking about) or dropping him off. I remember looking in my rearview mirror and seeing those infamous red and blue lights. My heart sank because I was also known for having a lead foot but on this particular day I wasn't speeding. I pull over and start to sweat a little at the same time just wondering what I had done. The officer comes up to the car and I roll down my window and the weirdest thing happened. He didn't ask me for my license or insurance, or even pull me over for anything in particular except to tell me and I quote "good game last week King". Let's just say being from Kansas City, Missouri I wasn't expecting that at all. I remember my face still being a little puzzled as I said, "thank you sir". All types of things were going through my mind like first how did you know this was my car, second how did you know that this was me in the car, and are police allowed to pull people over to say, "good game"? We talked for about 5 or 10 minutes about nothing but football when he said, "what are you averaging King about 3.5, 10, and 3"? I had never really kept up with my stats like that on the football field but assumed he was pretty close. At that moment, it dawned on me that I was averaging 3.5 sacks and 10 tackles per game as a Plainview Bulldog and it also dawned on me that I probably shouldn't get into any kind of trouble here because the town is small enough that they know you by name and car and they also have the power to pull you over and talk about football for a little while. But that was Texas for you, and Plainview to be more exact. They loved football down here and the talent that comes from smaller towns is still astonishing to me.

These kids have nothing to do but workout, and play sports and that's exactly what they did. Oh, and they love to drink too but we'll touch on that in a later chapter.

As good as people said I was at football, I still loved the game of basketball. In my mind, I'm just waiting for basketball season which took on a different direction as well. On the basketball court while I lived in Plainview, I only averaged 14 points and 8 rebounds which is decent but that wasn't getting any college scout's attention like my football stats were. In Kansas City, we had grown up together playing ball so we were like a family and each of us knew what the other could do. Here in Plainview, even though I could play ball, I was new here and just like me in Kansas City, these kids had grown up playing ball together and they were like a family and I'm the new kid on the block. My coaches back home who I had travelled with, and ate dinner with, and felt like a son to, knew how to bring out the best in me and here under a new basketball coach and a new system it was just all different. At times I felt like a fish out of water.

I was so caught up in being a basketball player that I didn't see or hear where God was taking me. In retrospect, I was given football as my pedestal to shine but I always chose basketball.

Metro High School Football Capsules

Posted: Friday, September 08, 2000

Amarillo High vs. Plainview

THE GAME: Amarillo High Sandies (1-0) vs. Plainview Bulldogs (0-1), 7:30 p.m. tonight, Bulldog Stadium, Plainview.

LAST WEEK: Amarillo High defeated Palo Duro 28-6; Plainview lost to El Paso Del Valle 47-34.

LAST MEETING: Amarillo High 28, Plainview 7 in 1997.

PLAYERS TO WATCH: For Plainview, quarterback Kyle Miller threw for 198 yards and two touchdowns in the Bulldogs' opener against EP Del Valle last week; running back Brylon Bradic rushed for 118 yards on 15 carries last week; defensive end Maurice King had three sacks and seven tackles against Del Valle.

My thoughts- In sports and even life, you are only as good as you are consistently good. I averaged crazy stats as a football player and decent stats as a basketball player. Don't get me wrong, there were some 30 point games and some 20+ point games scattered in there but I only averaged about 14 points and 8 rebounds. After the high school level, coaches want to know what you can do night in and night out. Having one good game here and another good game there is ok, however if you want to grab the attention of scouts you need to average decent numbers every game, home or away, sick or healthy and even hurt.

"NO MATTER WHAT YOU DO, YOU ARE ONLY AS GOOD AS YOU ARE CONSISTENTLY GOOD. PLAYERS LIKE KOBE, LEBRON, CURRY ETC. EVEN THOUGH THEY ARE EXCEPTIONAL TALENTS, THE COACH KNOWS EXACTLY WHAT HE IS GETTING FROM THESE PLAYERS EVERY GAME NO MATTER WHAT."   Maurice King

Things to think about

1. What do you average, every game?
2. What is an honest and realistic goal about what you need to average to gain notoriety from scouts and recruits?
3. Do you put in the work to average these numbers? Why not?
4. How consistent are you?

Chapter 7- Discipline, right place at the right time

By my senior year in high school things were going really well, I had adjusted to Texas and even began to like it, and I was also starting to get letters from tons of Div. 1 schools. I remember my parents having to take the phone off of the hook because it would literally ring all day from recruiting coaches who wanted to offer scholarships. I also remember having shoe boxes full of letters from schools like North Carolina, Texas Tech, Texas A&M, Baylor, Kentucky, Washington, TCU, Oregon, Kansas and a few more Div.1 schools which to any other kid would be awesome. I was excited don't get me wrong, but none of these letters were basketball letters, they all wanted me to come play football. My only reason for not committing to any of these schools were I just knew in my heart that I would get a call from a school that wanted me to play basketball and you guessed it, it never came.

Remember when I told you we would touch on the whole drinking thing in a later chapter? Well this is the chapter that I reluctantly have to tell you about both the biggest and worst day in my life as far as sports were concerned.

I remember it was a Wednesday because in Texas everybody went to church on Wednesday night. It was about 4 o'clock in the evening after school and my dad owned a store there called Faze 4 Sports, well apparently the head coach from Baylor University had come all the way to Plainview, Tx to see me. He walked in my dad's store after of coarse going to the high school and not finding me, so they tracked my dad down and walked into his store holding out a piece of paper. He didn't say hi, hello, how are you doing? or nothing. His words were as my dad told me, "I saw him on film and paper and I had to take a look at him with my own eyes. I have a 4-year scholarship right here and now if he wants to sign it". These were the days before cell phones were as big as they are now. I was able to disappear in a small town at the wrong time. It was 4 o'clock in the afternoon and I was out drinking with a group of friends. I wasn't ever a big drinker and at the time I really didn't know what I was doing or thinking for that matter. It was the end of my senior year and I was about to graduate with straight A's and I had also busted out a 1300 on my SAT scores out of a possible 1600 so to be honest I was in full party mode. In retrospect, there was a lot of things wrong on my part with that whole situation. First, who drinks at 4 o'clock in the afternoon in that Texas heat? Second, why was I even drinking as a high schooler? And third, if I had been where I was supposed to be, and doing what I was supposed to be doing my life would have gone an entire different direction as opposed to where it was about to go.

At this time, I was 6'5" about 285 pounds and ran a 4.49 40-yard dash time which is pretty good for a defensive end. I had the bright idea (being sarcastic) that I would lose 40 pounds to look and feel more like a basketball player and well, that was a mistake. Now the calls and letters that were once coming slowed down drastically. Again, I know it sounds redundant, but I was given football and I always chose basketball. After missing out on the Baylor and pretty much every other opportunity for football, time was running out and honestly, I was over the phone ringing and not knowing where I wanted to go and waiting on some magical basketball genie to grant my wish and allow me to play basketball at KU. One of my football coaches knocks on the door and brings a college coach in with him, he says those words again that honestly never really meant anything to me at the time, "we want you to play football for us and we are prepared to give you a scholarship". I just said yes with no research, no full understanding of what I said yes to or even what college I was saying yes to. At some point I found out that I was going to Cisco Jr. College, and I only agreed because they said I could play football and basketball.

My thoughts-This entire chapter was definitely a life defining moment for me. Had I been at the right place at the right time and doing what I was supposed to be doing I would have went to Baylor and had a good shot at going pro, or at the very least I could have graduated with a degree in something which would have also made my life after school a lot better. Had I only been disciplined or more disciplined than I was at that particular moment, maybe just maybe I could be in the stadium once again on Sundays but instead of in the stands I could be on the field. Who knows?

"ONE THING THAT ALL ATHLETES NEED TO KNOW IS, TALENT IS NEVER ENOUGH. YOU HAVE TO BE DISCIPLINED IN ALL AREAS OF YOUR LIFE FROM A MENTAL AND PHYSICAL ASPECT." Maurice King

King's jumper powers Plainview

Published: Saturday, January 27, 2001

PLAINVIEW Maurice King hit a 15-foot jump shot with approximately six seconds left Friday night, lifting Plainview past Estacado 49-47 and knocking the District 4-4A leading Matadors from the unbeaten ranks in league play.

PLAINVIEW 49, ESTACADO 47

Things to think about

1. What is discipline to you?
2. How much discipline towards you craft do you have if any?
3. What were the biggest mistakes that I made during this chapter and because of these mistakes what did I forfeit?

Chapter 8- Cisco Jr. College

Once again I found myself in a vehicle full of all of my belongings headed to a place where I really didn't want to be. But none the less I was going to college and for the first time I was going to be on my own. My first thought of Cisco Jr. College when I finally arrived was, this is definitely not Baylor. Cisco, Tx was located about halfway between Abilene, Tx and Ft. Worth, Tx and in this specific region at that specific time there was an onslaught of cricket mattings to the likes of which I had never experienced. Without exaggeration the ground was covered with a quarter-inch of crickets both dead and alive at all times. You literally couldn't take one step without hearing a crunch and when you looked at the light poles they were flying around them also. As I stood in line waiting to get my dorm assignment and key I looked at all of these huge football players from all over the country. Honestly, I didn't care if I could compete with them or not I just wanted to go home. Not back to Plainview, but all the way back to Kansas City. This was beneath me in every sense of the word, but I had placed myself in this situation and could only take responsibility for being there. My parents walked me to my dorm and helped me unload the car and set up my room. Crickets were in the dorms, the hallways, the showers and literally everywhere else you could imagine. I never told anybody this because of my pride and I was flat out too big to be crying but as my parents drove away, my eyes teared up heavily and it felt like the biggest frog in the world was lodged in my throat. And If I'm not mistaken I think my dad was laughing at me as he and my mom drove away.

I just wanted out of this place, but the funniest thing happened, I became the center of attention again and one more time I had to prove myself first as a football player and then as a basketball player. The next day was our first football practice and that's when I learned my first college level lesson. Conditioning goes to another level and for the most part everyone there is good. Here is a common misconception for

Jr. College sports. People think that because they are in Jr. College that they are not good and it's honestly the opposite. The talent in Jr. College is astounding, for the most part people are there not for lack of talent but in most cases lack of grades. I can remember my first college snap, we had a running back by the name of "smokey". I didn't know why people called him that but coaches, and even his parents called him "smokey" and I was about to find out why he had earned his nickname. I was always quick off of the ball but this is an honest account of how big an adjustment you had to make from high school to college. Smokey was about 4-5 yards behind the line of scrimmage where most running backs are in certain play sets. The quarterback said "hut" and by the time I stood out of my 3-point stance smokey was 10 yards past me heading into the linebacker/secondary part of our defense. My 1st thought was ok, now I know why and how he got that nickname, and my second thought was If I was going start for this team I had my work cut out for me. I earned a starting position but it didn't come easy as college on every level is a different animal than high school altogether and for the first time I had to work at the game of football.

After football season, according to our deal I walked into the basketball gym. I was a 6'5" forward who could dribble and shoot and there stood in front of me 6'8" forwards and 6'7" guards and everything in between. I was smiling as now I was right where I wanted to be but that smile quickly disappeared. Remember college conditioning is on an entire different level. Coach Cornish loaded up two vans and drove us 10 miles outside of town and it wasn't to show us the scenery if any that Cisco had to offer. He told us to get out and jog back. I prayed he was joking but he wasn't. So all 10 of us jogged back to the campus and here is where it got even worse. Cisco Jr. College sits on top of a hill, so after a 10 mile jog we now had to run up this mountain of a hill and then have a two-hour college level basketball practice. Once again everyone on the college level is good at something, that's why they are there. I know it doesn't look like that on the t.v. screen but trust me everyone for the most part is good.

I had successfully made the transition from high school athlete to college athlete and believe it or not, everyone can't make this transition easily and I didn't make it easily but I made it. I also made another life altering decision and I quit football altogether and once again focused only on basketball. Why did I do that?

My thoughts- I was so driven by basketball that I drove completely out of my destiny. I chose to walk away from the very thing that earned me a college scholarship in the first place. I was still in my own way trying to get that paper that I didn't get way back in the 5th or 6th grade but this time it didn't work in my favor.

“SOMETIMES LIFE IS EASY AND WE MAKE IT HARD”
Maurice King

Things to think about

1. On what level is your conditioning? Do you condition for the level you are at, or for the level you are going?
2. Even though I initially missed out on the Baylor opportunity, could I have still gotten there from Jr. College had I done the right things?
3. Transition is a part of life, but as an athlete can you make the transition from High School to College and then from College to

the Pro's? How do you play when everyone around you is as good or better than you?

Players of The Week Honorable Mention

Posted: Tuesday, October 03, 2000

Class 4A

Plainview defensive tackle Maurice King made 11 tackles, recorded two sacks, caused one fumble and returned an interception 54 yards for a touchdown during the Bulldogs' 35-21 District 4-4A-opening win

Chapter 9- Knowing where I was going, finding myself

In this chapter and the following chapters are the real reason and motivation for writing this book. It was never my goal to write about any accomplishment that I had reached, rather only to bring us to the point of the story where we are now.

I flunked out of Cisco Jr. College and that was the beginning of the end of my career as an athlete. I bounced around after that, but grades or the lack there of, kept coming back to haunt me. I walked on and made the team at North Western Oklahoma State University and a few more colleges but could never master the art of not having somebody to tell me to do my homework and get it turned in, as well as not having anyone there to make sure I was coming in at a decent hour. College became an all-out party to the point where I was coming in at the hours where most were going to work or class. And I also managed to create a beautiful baby girl with another basketball star on the college level at Texas Tech University. For me at that point it was over, I now had to create an identity outside of sports which was altogether new because from 6 or 7 years of age I was an athlete on one level or another. I spent the next 15 years of my life trying to figure out who and what I was.

I had never thought for one second that I wouldn't make it professionally playing a sport. When you don't know where you are going ultimately in life a lot of things can go awry and usually when things can go awry they most certainly always do. I found myself doing and selling drugs, and just caught in a life where I was never really meant to be. It was by the grace of God that I did not go to jail or worse because of the things that I was doing. I was lost in a world that at one time seemed so promising. How could I go from bright future to future felon? To make a long story short, it was because I had no direction, I didn't go to college with any other intention other than playing basketball and football. In retrospect, I probably should have studied a major that would allow me to become a coach because I have always been able coach the game and inspire others as well. It wasn't until the age of 30 that I found who and what I was. See the first part of my life I was running from what God created me to be, and I will spend the rest of my life running towards what God created me to be which is entrepreneur and motivational speaker (Just like my father again). I think life, even though nobody is exempt from ups and downs and struggles of one form or another can be quite easy but we make it hard. Maybe I'm speaking for myself, but from the beginning of my life I never really listened to what God was telling me because I could only hear and see what I wanted to hear and see and in some crazy way while I chased that crazy little paper that I never got in 6th grade for basketball I had over-looked all of the papers so-to-speak that God gave me for football. I had allowed the same thing that set me apart, be the same thing to tear me apart.

My thoughts- As athletes, we get so caught up in "making it" that we are blinded to the fact of even if we do make it playing professionally, one day at one time or another your career will be over as an athlete because no one can play the game forever. And if by chance you don't have an identity outside of sports, you can spend a lot of time trying to figure out or create one. Again, had I started with what I was naturally gifted and great at, I could have saved myself a lot of time, heartache and pain.

Maurice King

Things to think about

1. Do you have a written out plan for your life that you look at everyday? Is this important and why?
2. What would you like to major in during college?
3. What are some professions outside of sports that you have thought about pursuing? What is a good age to know what you want to do in life?

Chapter 10- Sometimes it's easy and we make it hard

Looking back on life as a 34 year old man, I made a ton of mistakes. Yes everything, both good and bad molded me into the person that I am now however it didn't have to be so complicated. There is a gray area in life and a lot of people struggle with this concept. There is a difference between being stubborn in the pursuit of your goals and standing in the way of them. Time after time in my life God was giving me the keys to success and I let a love for something that I was never destined to become get in the way of what I was created to be. As a teenager, I was the size of a lot professional football players and never realized that until my senior year in high school that I never once worked at the game of football I was just naturally talented and gifted. In your pursuit of greatness, start where you are naturally gifted because those are God-given abilities in whatever that may be. As a coach, I tell my kids all of the time, if you are trying to figure out who and what you are you must be strong enough and honest enough to look in the mirror and decide what it is you see. For me I looked in the mirror and saw a football player dying to play the game of basketball and others saw a talented basketball player but a great football player who was never committed to football. I now have 3 beautiful kids, who are talented at different things and as they begin to discover and find out who and what they are I pray that they listen to the obvious and be driven by the goals they have set for themselves but don't over-look what God has given them because that is always the best place to start the search. I'm not sure If I would do it over if I could, maybe it was my purpose to go through that so that someone else wouldn't. I guess I'll never know, but what I find funny is that I sub-consciously mimic all of the coaches I have ever had and If I can make them (my players) better men and women, then I have accomplished something greater than any award, or trophy could present. I learned a lot from the games of football and basketball, but most importantly I learned that just like Coach Kahlil told us in 5th or 6th grade, "playing sports is a great way to learn life because there will always be another practice or game, but you only get one shot at life". I now know what he meant by that on several different levels.

As a coach now, every now and again I lace up my shoes and put on that head band and get out there with the kids to show them that I know what I'm talking about. And like clock-work there is always one kid who wants to challenge my ability to play the game, and all of a sudden I feel that "perfect storm" of competitiveness start rumbling inside of me. Of coarse, I demolish all of my opponents even though they are kids and as I'm now 34 and not in any type of playing shape I'm sore for the next 3 days but the love will never die if it's in fact true love.

My thoughts-Your love and drive for something should wake you up in the morning. When someone is dedicated to something such as a sport or anything in life for that matter, they sacrifice and do what they have to do to succeed even if it means less sleep, or lost friends, or not having the type of social life that other friends seem to have. One should be so focused that it almost becomes tunnel-vision in pursuit of their desired goal. Without excuse, a golfer for example can golf on any coarse, in any weather condition or situation because of his love for the game and desire to be great. There are no excuses.

"LIFE IS EASY, BUT WE CHOOSE TO MAKE IT HARD"
Maurice King

Things to think about

1. What are some characteristics that all great athletes have in common?
2. How important is belief in yourself?
3. What do you believe that God is telling you about who you are and what you are?

Chapter 11- Acknowledgments

There is a list of people who I want to thank for all that was poured into me at all stages of my life. In no particular order, I want to thank all of my coaches growing up. Coach Kahlil for instilling mental toughness and Coach Ronnie for both not giving me my paper, then giving me my paper after I earned it. It was because of you that I started my development as an athlete. I want to thank Coach Mark Hollins for seeing things in me when nobody else did and making me play like a grown man in a child's body. I also want to thank you for being like a father to me as well and never taking it easy on me at all. I want to thank Coach Kevin Morris for also seeing what I could become and allowing me room to grow into that. I want to thank Coach Don Bickham for being that "no-nonsense" coach that showed me the mentality I would have to have in order to play at any level after high school. I want to thank my dad Danny Clark who showed me the off-season attitude of an elite athlete and last but not least my mother Jacqueline Clark who taught me my first lessons as an athlete and grew with me, and made sure I had shoes and cleats and made it to practices and games after working 50 and 60 hours a week. I look back and think of all the money that you had to pay just so I could play what I loved to play and even though I didn't make it pro, those lessons and character building moments are priceless. I also want to thank all of the teammates I had during these times. We won together, lost together, cried together and ran sprints together (disciplinary action) but I wouldn't change a thing.

From the bottom of my heart- THANK YOU

I almost forgot about my sisters and brother. Chelle was my sister that kind of became everyone else's sister because most times when you saw me, you saw her. (or heard her) lol. I also want to thank Portia and Gary for being there with and for me growing up as well and also allowing me to coach the game that I always have and always will love.

It was because of all of you in the above mentioned that I was able to play with, for, or against people in the likes of Bob Knight(Coach), Tubby Smith(Coach), Lex Lugar(Wrestler), Andre Emitt (Texas Tech, Seattle Super Sonics, Overseas), Jason McNiel (China) and a host of other players who made it playing their dream and will confirm that I gave them all a run for their money. And also that I was able to receive various awards (my paper)

(if I left you out please forgive me as it was not intentional in any way, shape, form or fashion.)

All newspaper articles were provided and or written by

<u>Amarillo Globe News</u>

<u>Plainview Daily Herald</u>

<u>Lubbock Avalanche Journal</u>

I dedicate this book to all who have come before me and all that will come after me in hopes of making it professionally in any sport. I pray that you can capitalize off of my strengths and learn from my mistakes and my story. If this book can reach and positively alter the life of just one athlete then not only have I succeeded but in a sense we have succeeded together.

Maurice King